And he will turn
The hearts of the fathers to the children,
And the hearts of the children to their fathers,
Lest I come and strike the earth with a curse.
Malachi 4:6 NKJV

□ *Steps to Manhood*

James E. Warren □

Steps to Manhood: The Making of a Mentor

3

□ *Steps to Manhood*

Since the beginning of time, mothers have nurtured and sacrificed for their children. Mothers have always provided unconditional love and support to their children. However, it takes a village to raise a child. Our mothers need help. They need men to be mentors to their sons as they take their steps to manhood. There are men in every city who work diligently to make a difference in the lives of boys. These men serve our communities without funding or public acknowledgment for their service. They are motivated by the desire to offer hope to the next generation. The future of our nation rests in the hands of men who are willing to serve our youth as mentors. It is to these men that this book is dedicated.

□ *Steps to Manhood*

Table of Contents

Introduction

After years of participating in sports, I was asked to coach a youth basketball team. It soon became clear that I was coaching much more than basketball. I was coaching life. Although the boys I worked with had devoted mothers caring for them, they were crying out for a man's perspective. They wanted a man to show them the way on their journey to manhood. I observed that they needed to be affirmed and loved by an adult male. Sometimes, when boys feel unloved, they become violent. As a result, Chicago has been compared to a nation devastated by war because of the amount of violence in our communities. I *had to step* in and do what I could.

These observations were confirmed during my years in ministry. While serving as the president of a men's ministry at a large urban church, I noticed the absence of men in the home, the church and the community. **Let me be clear: I am not saying that single mothers cannot raise boys! There are many outstanding mothers successfully raising their sons. I am suggesting that we provide an opportunity to support single mothers who desire additional help.**

Much later, many of the players from my coaching days came back to thank me for giving them an alternative to wandering the streets. Over time, these experiences led to the creation of Center for Community Development, NFP (CCD) and our male mentoring program, Steps to Manhood. CCD is a 501c(3) non-profit organization committed to the development of youth, the empowerment of men, and the promotion of economic development. Because every boy needs hope, the curriculum for Steps to Manhood Mentoring is designed to offer hope through training in life skills, character development, financial literacy and entrepreneurship. By preparing boys to be responsible men, they become assets to their family and community, instead of casualties of a fatherless culture.

In the pages that follow, I will review how I was mentored, how I became a mentor and how the non-profit Center for Community Development and Steps to Manhood Mentoring came into being.

The Battle Against the African American Family and the Need to Mentor Young Men

Artillery shells lie scattered on the ground while the evening sky shines bright like noonday. The battle is raging. This battleground is located in the hearts and minds of urban youth. Like a soldier in the heat of battle, the American family is fighting for its life, particularly the African American family. The enemy has surrounded the family. One by one the opposing army is eliminating members of the family unit. This is not a fictional account. Families in general and African-American families in particular are under siege. Our battle cry is, "Save our boys!"

The Cycle of Despair

Let me give you an example. I met Nathan[1] years ago when he was a young man, and I was a basketball coach. Over the years I came to find out he had multiple brushes with the law and had been arrested several times. Of course, he didn't tell me this at the beginning. Many young men are not forthcoming about their in-

---

[1]   Names have been changed throughout to protect privacy.

13

carceration experiences because of shame, and Nathan was no exception.

As time passed, Nathan grew up and fathered sons and daughters. But he wasn't in the home to be a dad to his kids. Because of lack of employment, he remained outside the home.

You may wonder why lack of employment would cause a father to be absent from his home. Shame is the answer. Men are too ashamed to face their families when they are unable to provide for them. Over the years I've tried to explain to men that their children need them more than they need anything material that they might provide. But overcoming shame is a part of the culture that changes slowly.

I know Nathan's children. Over the years, I've seen them struggle with anger and disciplinary issues. Why? Because they don't have a dad in their lives.

Nathan desires to work, but like many others who never attended college or trade school, he is unable to find meaningful employment. His story is prototypical. Unable to find work that will support his family, he bounces around, struggles financially, and finally resorts to a life of crime. In his eyes, he's "hustling" which he views as positive. But, by selling marijuana or whatever the drug and/or contraband of demand may be, he's simply breaking the law in the eyes of society. What he views as positive is seen as negative by the society in which he lives.

Why don't things change for Nathan? One major reason is this: He doesn't ask for help. Why not? Shame is part of the answer. But another part is that he just doesn't know how to ask for help.

Help for Nathan needs to come in the right form. You could give him an ideal job today, but he would probably lose it tomorrow. Growing up without guidance, without a dad and without mentors, he lacks the basic life skills to hold down a good job that would provide for his family. He needs to be taught human relations and other life skills that would give him the maturity to handle the high level of responsibility he and his family need.

This is the role a father should fulfill, but there are precious few fathers in the African American community. This is why mentors are desperately needed. Young men need surrogate dads.

Nathan has experienced a lifetime of rejection and disappointment on many levels. He was rejected by his dad, by his girlfriends, by his children. He's been in and out of institutions. For so long he has not been selected for employment that along with many others like him, he just stopped trying.

The best time to intervene with someone like Nathan is when he is a young man. I'm determined to give young men like him the hope and skills needed to bridge the gap between where they are and where they could be.

Statistics Tell the Story

Is Nathan an isolated anomaly? Not at all.

When reporting on this subject, the *New York Times* brought up the example of a man who "quit school in 10th grade to sell drugs, fathered four children with three mothers, and spent several stretches in jail for drug possession, parole violations and other crimes." They called it "a story so commonplace it hardly bears notice."[2] Statistics bear this out. In Chicago, only 30% of Black male public high school students graduate by their 18th birthday. Only 10% of the Black and Latino male students earn a 4-year college degree by the time they become adults.[3] Black males are disproportionately labeled as discipline and behavioral problems then fast-tracked out of high school through expulsions and suspensions.[4] Unemployment rates for Black American youth are three times higher than the national average.[5] Black men who graduate from high school earn from 25% to 35% more than black men who drop out.[6] About one third of black male high school dropouts aged 22 to 30 were incarcerated in 2000. Only 3.3 percent of White male dropouts the same age were behind bars.[7] For every 2.6 young Black

---

[2] http://www.nytimes.com/2006/03/20/national/20blackmen. html?pagewanted=all&_r=0 Daniel Bassill is founder / CEO of Tutor / Mentor Institute with 40 years of mentoring experience.

[3] University of Chicago Consortium on Chicago School Research

[4] Georgia's African American Male Initiative

[5] National Black United Fund

[6] U.S. Bureau of the Census, 1997

[7] Stanford Report, 2005

men in college, there is one in jail, while for young White males, the college to jail ratio is 28 to 1.[8]

Today, 24.7 million children are living in father-absent houses;[9] that is, one out of every three children in America lives in homes where their father does not live. Children who grow up in father-absent homes are significantly more likely to have a turbulent childhood. 75% of American children from single-parent homes will experience poverty by the time they turn 11 years old, compared to only 20% for families with two parents. Violent criminals are predominately males from homes where the father was absent, including 72% of adolescent murderers and 70% of long-term prison inmates. Children of father-absent homes are more likely to be suspended from school, or drop out; commit suicide as adolescents; and, are frequently victims of child abuse or neglect.[10]

The only way to fix the violence in Chicago, according to Daniel Bassill,[11] is for a new group of community leaders to emerge. Bassill points to the scant progress made in addressing this problem since the October 1992 Chicago *SunTimes* front page photo of a seven year old boy shot as he walked to school in the Cabrini-Green neighborhood. He asks the question, "How do

---

[8] US Department of Justice
[9] Father Facts
[10] Just the Facts: A Summary of Rent information of America's Children and their Families, 1993
[11] Bassill, Daniel, "More Shot in Chicago? What's the Solution?" Online article dated 10/15/2014. https://www.linkedin.com/pulse/article/20141015144302-5205770-more-shot-in-chicago-what-s-the-solution accessed 12/1/2014.

we move beyond the prayers, marches and flag-lowering, to the research, planning, brainstorming and action steps that are needed?"

We achieve meaningful and lasting solutions, Bassill argues, with community volunteers who bring together several qualities: They take the time to educate themselves on the real root causes of violence. They network with others to spread awareness and understanding. They offer to help without waiting to be asked. They choose a neighborhood and use their strengths to make a difference. They build a shared understanding. They sacrificially give of their time and money to make a difference. In his article, Bassill connects violence, poor school performance and poverty. He places a strong accent on tutoring and mentoring as tools in the hands of community volunteers to effectively address the root causes of violence.

Problems Created by Absent Fathers / Dysfunctional Homes

The hole created by the absence of fathers can be seen in many segments of society. Several ladies at my church have expressed the deep longing they feel for the love of their fathers. Studies have shown that the relationship children have with their fathers impacts their relationships as adults with other adults.[12] For example, when men are absent from the lives of their daughters, the girls experience difficulties establishing

---

[12] Report to Congress on Out-of-Wedlock Childbearing, 1995

relationships with men. As adult women, they miss the example of love and respect fathers provide for their daughters. The father and daughter relationship prepares women to select a husband.

When men are absent from the lives of their sons, as adults they experience difficulties with authority figures. Fathers equip boys with tools they will need later in life. They demonstrate (model) the way a man should treat others, especially in the employer or employee relationship. Additionally, boys watch the way their fathers treat their mothers. This relationship influences the way boys interact with the girls and women in their lives. If a boy sees his father physically abuse his mother, he will often grow up and manifest the same behaviors. The son, now a man, will abuse his wife. After repeated abuse, the spouse usually will decide to leave her husband. Consequently, the dysfunctional husband-wife relationship fragments the family and serves as the blueprint for future relationships. This blueprint is the construction plan for building a dysfunctional family. And, when a construction company builds on a faulty foundation, the building eventually crumbles. Broken families will create broken communities. As a boy growing up in Chicago, I saw the obstacles that impede the development of urban kids—family disintegration, poverty, drug addiction, violence and promiscuity.

Why Are Fathers Absent from the Home?

Why are fathers absent from the home? They are not present in the home for any of the following four reasons:

(1) *Substance abuse.* Alcohol and other drug abuse and addictions keep dads from the kind of stability needed to assume their responsibilities in the home. They can even be physically present but mentally and emotionally absent.

(2) *Lack of employment.* Men want to be providers, and when they cannot provide, they feel like they are less than a man. They would rather not allow their children to see them as inadequate. I try to encourage them that their *presence* in the home is more important than their *presents.* First and foremost, their children need them, not the things they might provide. "You're more important than money in the bank," I say. But with so much self-worth tied to economics, men feel a deep sense of shame if they cannot provide. In addition, many who are unable to find employment turn to selling drugs and/or contraband for a living.

(3) *Incarceration.* As the statistics indicate, a disproportionate number of African American males are in jail or prison. Many of these are for non-violent drug sales and drug possession.

(4) *Tumultuous relationships* with their children's mother. Many men, having never had a loving marriage modeled to them, simply don't know how to handle the challenges of an intimate relationship. Unfortunately,

the children wind up becoming collateral damage.

Dwindling Employment in the Inner City

Once upon a time, manufacturing jobs were available to those who didn't have advanced schooling. Men could earn a livable wage in a manufacturing plant. But, as more and more of these jobs move off shore, opportunities for high school dropouts—and even high school graduates—dwindle. Corporate mergers over the last two decades have also eroded the number of available entry level positions for unskilled and/or semi-skilled individuals.

Of course, many young men start college, but never finish because they can't handle the independence. In their short sightedness, they party their opportunity away. As a result, they have not equipped themselves with the credentials needed for the employment opportunities that remain.

Peer Mentoring

College is one place where peer mentoring makes a huge difference. In my own case, peer mentoring and motivation started while I was at Chicago's Hales Franciscan High School. At this private parochial school for African American males, the atmosphere was competitive, but friendly. We loved a challenge. The higher the bar, the more we strove to reach it. In the meanwhile, we supported and encouraged one another toward our individual goals.

This spirit continued on into college. One of my best friends kept saying to me, "I'm here on a scholarship. I need to keep a 3.20 GPA to keep my scholarship. There's no way my grandparents can pay this tuition. I gotta study." His example encouraged me to study as well. We encouraged each other to reach graduation.

In this peer mentoring atmosphere, I developed friendships with many young men and those friendships continue to today, thirty, nearly forty years later. These men have become teachers, attorneys, CPAs, a feature sportswriter, an MD, and a vice president of a major corporation.

This is a missing link for many young men. They have peers whose influence is more negative than positive. I tell the young men that I mentor, "If you're the smartest man in the group you're traveling in, you need to get another group." The Biblical writer of Proverbs says, "As iron sharpens iron, so one man sharpens another."[13] Plastic doesn't sharpen iron (you need iron to sharpen iron).

I need to emphasize here that I'm not just talking about intelligence. I'm talking about character. It takes character and integrity to hold down a job, to stay in a marriage, to be a daddy to children and to manage money well. So many of the things that are needed for stability trace directly back to character.

---

[13]   Proverbs 27:17 LEB

The Development of a Mentor

"Mentoring is a lifetime investment in our children that benefits the community."

Matilda Raffa Cuomo, founder and chairperson of Mentoring USA (1995)

How I Became Interested in Mentoring

In 1988, after years of participating in sports, I was asked to coach a youth basketball team. After accepting the invitation, I volunteered to serve as the assistant basketball coach at South Shore Baptist Church.[14] After my first year of coaching, I became the head coach. We gathered high school students who did not play high school basketball into the church. They came twice a week for a Bible lesson and then basketball practice. But, when our time together was over, I could see they still had needs—deep needs that were going unmet. Many of those needs were the result of the absence of fathers and the absence of hope. Perhaps it was my God-given gifts of mercy and helps—maybe it was the fact that I was a dad myself, but I looked on these boys as though they were my own sons. They needed character development, integrity, responsibility and life skills. Many of them had innate entrepreneurial skills, but, without the right kind of coaching, they would channel those skills for the wrong purposes.

It was in this context that my desire to be a mentor to young men in the African American community coa-

---

[14] Name later changed to Christ Bible Church

lesced. But as I reviewed my own life experiences, I began to see that my journey into mentoring actually started much earlier.

My Great-Great-Grandfather

The seeds of service to my community were planted by John Wesley Hawkins, my great-great-grandfather. He used his skill as a carpenter to develop communities in the state of Louisiana. He built several churches in and around Princeton, Louisiana. Many of those churches still exist today.

My Father

My father, Rev. Franklin Warren, was one of twelve children born to my grandmother. But my dad's father was killed before he was born, so he grew up without his biological father. Without having that male role model in his life, my dad did the best he could. He wasn't perfect, but he was certainly honest and transparent. He never pretended to be someone he wasn't. If he had a shortcoming, he admitted it. If he wasn't good at something, he simply said, "You'll need to learn about this; I'm not good at it."

My grandmother rallied around my dad to ensure that he received a formal education. My dad desired to be an educated pastor, so he attended and graduated from Vanderbilt Divinity School in Nashville, Tennessee before entering the ministry full-time. Rather than approaching church leadership like a traditional Southern Baptist African American preacher, he was more of an expositor, a teacher. Since my mother's father was a Christian Methodist Episcopal (CME) pastor, my dad started in the same denomination. Later he became a pastor in the Presbyterian and the United Methodist churches before finally coming back to the CME.

I am the youngest of four children, having two older brothers and an older sister. When I was a young child, my parents' marriage was beginning to fall apart. I felt like there was something I could have done to make things better. But, of course, at my young age I was powerless to change that part of my world. When I was seven years old, my parents divorced. I wrestled with feeling that I had done something to cause the divorce. It was a very confusing time for me however both of my parents were an encouragement to me.

When I was a young child, our family lived in the parsonage of the Presbyterian church at which my dad was pastor. After the divorce, my mom bought a home for us and the four of us remained with her. My dad lived twenty minutes away, near the Hyde Park area where President Obama has his home.

When husbands divorce their wives, they often "divorce" their children as well. But my dad never went that route. He never gave up on me. This has inspired in me a commitment to relationships—to never give up on my own children and others who are under my care. My dad and I remained close, especially as I grew older. When I reached the age of eleven or twelve—on the threshold of becoming a young man, I started to ask the question: *What did my dad like to do when he was my age?* Even though I lived with my mother, I wanted to reach out to my father and strengthen that relationship. I visited him most weekends.

My dad and I also related around sports, though in a very different way. My dad was from Oklahoma near the Texas border, and he loved football. When I was eleven or twelve years old, he wanted to see what I could do with a football in my hands. To my great surprise, I was able to elude him and run past the goal line. I didn't imagine I could do it. It was a wonderful bonding moment for both of us.

After my parents divorced, my dad became a chaplain at the University of Chicago Hospitals. As I grew up, I caught the bus and we met at the University of Chicago on Sundays. I watched him minister to sick patients at one of the University hospitals. I wheeled patients into the chapel where my dad conducted services. After the services were over, since he didn't cook, we ate at a restaurant not far from where he lived. One day, long before I had my driver's license, he wasn't feeling well so he asked me if I knew how to drive. I had watched him drive hundreds of times, so I said yes. "Okay," he said, "drive us home." Somehow we made it home in one piece with me at the wheel, and it became another bonding experience for us. It stuck with me.

I attended Hales Franciscan High School, the only all-male African American high school in the state of Illinois. The motto of this nationally acclaimed Catholic school was *"in virum perfectum"* or "unto perfect manhood." My high school was within walking distance of where my dad lived, so we often shared lunch together or went to high school sporting events together.

Even though they divorced, my parents remained reasonably cordial with one another. One thing I deeply appreciated about my dad is this: He never said a negative word to me about my mom. Instead, when he spoke of her, he praised her.

Throughout his life my dad suffered from epilepsy but he never wanted people to know. He believed potential employers would consider him unfit to perform the required duties. Despite the challenges my dad faced over the course of his lifetime, he was never bitter.

When I was a college student—about twenty or twenty-one years old, Dad went back to being a chaplain, this time in the prisons near Plymouth, Michigan. I later found, among my dad's possessions, cards of appreciation from many of those inmates.

Since my brothers and sister have wrestled with health issues most of their lives, as my parents have aged, most of the responsibility for their care has rested on me. As my dad grew older, his health was failing, and he needed help. Not only was he an epileptic, but he was taking longer and longer to recover from his seizures. In addition, he wasn't walking well. He eventually asked me to take over his finances. For some time my wife and I would make the three and a half hour drive from Chicago to Jackson, Michigan at least once a month to check on him and make sure his bills were paid, he was receiving his medication, and was otherwise okay. Eventually, we moved him to the Chicago area so he could be closer to his children and grandchildren. Toward the end, when we went to see him, he thanked me for being there for him. When people asked him questions about his finances, he took pride in saying, "I don't handle that. Talk to my son."

My Dad's Legacy of Affirmation

My dad passed away in March of 2012. However, his legacy lives on in my life through the many lessons he taught me. Here are a few examples.

I often worked as a volunteer at my father's side, transporting patients in the hospital to the chapel for worship services and for prayer. This experience created in me a lifelong desire to serve others.

When I was at the critical ages of ten, eleven and twelve, I watched everything my dad did. I can't imagine how difficult it must be for other young people who don't have dads in their lives. As I've reflected on what I gained in my own childhood, I've developed a deep inner burden to help young males—particularly those who don't have a father in their lives—to make the transition from boyhood to manhood. I also understand that boys need men to help them make that transition. As important as mothers and sisters and other females are, no one can take the place of a man in a boy's life.

The contrast between my experience and the experience of many of my peers has reinforced for me this reality: Rebuilding our communities means bringing fathers back into homes. Children need their fathers. The Biblical prophet Malachi speaks of this in the last verse of the Old Testament of the Bible: "And he shall turn the heart of the fathers to the children, and the heart of the children to their fathers, lest I come and smite the earth with a curse."[15]

I've become an advocate for mentoring but I also realize that no one can take the place of a dad. As a mentor, I don't try. In fact, I tell my mentees, "I'm not trying to usurp your dad's position or authority in your life. Consider me an older brother. I'm on your team. I'm your cheerleader."

I don't pity the people I mentor. Instead, I encourage them and give them motivation. I empathize, but I don't pity. Young people don't need or want pity they want someone who cares for them and cares about their well-being.

As I was growing up, my dad and I often played one-on-one basketball. During one of my first games I thought he would let me score, but when I went to shoot, there he was, standing over me. It was a teachable moment, and he used it to say to me, "Anything you get in life, son, you earn." That stayed with me my entire life. I never expected anyone to give me anything. But I did expect to have an opportunity to earn my own way. I watched both my parents go to work every day, and I do the same. This is a value that I've worked

---

[15]   Malachi 4:6 KJV

29

to pass on to my three sons who are now in their teens and early twenties.

While my dad claimed no skill at managing money, he praised my mom for her abilities in that area. He often said to me, "Learn how to manage your money like your mom." By following that advice, I developed a lifelong interest in financial literacy. I also became interested in teaching young people to develop the character and life skills to be financially responsible. I helped others connect with competent people who could help them with estate planning and investments. I observed the close connection between good character and getting a good job, integrity and managing money well. I also understand that once someone enters their fifties, it's difficult to enter the job market—most employers won't want to pay a livable wage. So people also need the wherewithal to create their own business. By teaching these skills, I've been able to impart hope and options to young men.

Sue Duncan

Sue Duncan[16] was born into privilege and raised in affluence in the Boston area. Although her mother was not warm, Sue received loving care throughout her childhood from an African American nanny. After growing up and marrying a University of Chicago professor, she decided to give back what she received from her nanny. Though still in her twenties, at her own ex-

---

[16] Mother of Arne Duncan, US Secretary of Education under President Barack Obama.

pense,[17] she drove into a "war zone"—one of the most gang-infested, challenging neighborhoods in Chicago, determined to make a difference.

For the next fifty years this white woman became a fixture in that African American neighborhood. In 1961, despite death threats and harassment, she established the Sue Duncan Children's Center, a place for tutoring neighborhood children. As her mission became known, the community embraced her, and her daily arrival was cause for celebration. Like clockwork, she drove her blue Suburban slowly down the street at the same time each day, with children running alongside it looking forward to a snack, tutoring and love.

I knew nothing about this until I was nine years old. While I grew up on the south side of Chicago in a safe, nurturing community, my cousins lived in the high crime, gang infested neighborhood where Sue Duncan worked. When I was nine, I spent the summer with cousins. One day, standing on the balcony of my aunt's third floor apartment on Woodlawn Avenue, my cousins spotted Sue's Suburban coming down the street. They started yelling, "Sue's coming! Sue's coming!" Then they raced to see who could run the fastest to Sue's Center. I was left on the balcony wondering, *Who is Sue? Why are my cousins so eager to see her?* Because a young mind wanted to know, I asked my aunt for permission to attend Sue's Center.

Warm but firm, Sue Duncan's approach was to provide opportunities for those who didn't have the advantages

---

[17]   She funded her program with her own inheritance.

that others enjoyed. Sue created a safe and encouraging environment for all the children under her care. The Center was comfortable, like a second home. Sue, and her family, made me feel like I was a part of their family. Knowing that many children came to the Center hungry, she prepared delicious, nutritious snacks. When the students she tutored complained that they couldn't do something she challenged them to do it, her reply was always the same, "Yes, you can, and I'm going to help you. Yes, you can, and you will." She insisted that everyone give their best effort. She organized the students so that the older ones were helping the younger ones. Everything was well thought out. Children were eager to please her, and, of course, everyone wanted to participate in gym time after tutoring ended. No child wanted to hear, "You weren't following instructions; you don't get to go to gym."[18] By providing a safe haven of hope for children, Sue Duncan was a minister of mercy to children in need. Through caring, nurturing and mentoring, she helped thousands to become better students. Countless individuals went on to college and beyond. She inspired thousands of people, and her center was at least partially responsible for a plethora of success stories. Among the many people who went through her program and went on to achieve success in life was Michael Clarke Duncan, the actor in the movie *The Green Mile*. Michael's success in Hollywood did not prevent him from crediting the SDCC for putting him on a path to success.

---

[18] Sue Duncan's Children's Center was the only safe place in that area where a child could play indoors for free. All other gyms required a membership or entrance fee.

I went from being a student in her program to being a reading and math literacy volunteer years later during my summers home from college. My church developed a similar program, and her program helped to inspire me to establish the Center for Community Development, NFP (CCD) in 2004.

Sue Duncan is now in the early stages of Alzheimer's. Others have taken over the task of funding and operating her center. But she continues to be a much loved "mother" in a community that needed love.

Hales Franciscan High School

I arrived at Hales Franciscan High School, an all-male African American Catholic institution, as an extremely shy freshman.

Because this was an all male high school, there was plenty of testosterone. Every student needed to prove himself. I was constantly being challenged. While my natural response was to walk away, I got to the point where I needed to assert myself, or I would be challenged every day. For me this started with athletics. I needed to learn to face and overcome challenges.

During that first year, I was presented with opportunities to try out for teams, to run for student government positions—in short to set goals and achieve them. For example, I tried out for the freshman basketball team. Competition was fierce. Several of my peers came into the program having been recruited to the high school by athletic talent scouts. But I had learned from my dad that I needed to work hard to earn my place in life. So I worked hard. I also noticed how frustrated the coach became when his requests and instructions were ignored by the other students. I determined that I would be different; I would be coachable. As a result, I went from just another kid in the crowd to a starter on the team. When I was placed on the team, the coach could rely on me to follow his instructions. This reinforced for me the importance of listening. Today, when I'm mentoring young men, I tell them, "I won't talk to you for an hour; you get that all day. Instead, I'm going to listen to you, and you're going to hear from me."

The lessons I learned on the basketball court soon transferred to the classroom. Although I performed well in school, I was very reticent about speaking out or taking initiative. I tended to sit in the back of the class, and say nothing. But as the teachers called on me and realized I knew the answers, they encouraged me to speak out. The teachers and coaches there helped me to gain a voice and become more comfortable and confident in sharing my thoughts. I became more actively involved in moving to the front, raising my hand, participating and accepting any challenge I was given.

While my freshman year helped me come out of my shell, I learned a valuable lesson during my years as an upperclassman. At that time in my life, I tended to worry quite a bit. On one particular occasion, I was worried about an examination, even though I had studied and prepared for it. One of my instructors said to me, "Has the Lord ever let you down?" For me that was a light bulb moment. I realized that here I was a preacher's kid, and it had not occurred to me to pray about my schooling or about the things that made me anxious. I realized that I had the option of processing the difficulties I was experiencing with God in prayer.

The training I received at Hales prepared me to overcome the setbacks that were to come in my life. Hales Franciscan High School had prepared me academically, personally, and socially to make an impact for Christ in my community.

The experience at Hales had a lasting impact on my life and ministry. The school motto, "unto perfect manhood," became the template for my mentoring program, Steps to Manhood. A bible passage that embodies both my high school experience and the mentoring program is 1 Corinthians 13:11, "When I was a child, I spoke as a child; I understood as a child, I thought as a child: but when I became a man, I put away childish things." (NKJV) High school helped me understand that we need to take steps to reach that manhood, and that character transformation needs to take place to move from thinking childish thoughts to thinking adult thoughts.

A Near Miss

Another defining moment occurred when I was eighteen years old. I had just obtained my driver's license,[19] and I was driving the family to Oklahoma when one of

---

[19] I was unable to take driver's education so I needed to postpone getting my license until I was eighteen.

the rear tires blew out. I was totally unprepared for this and barely managed to safely bring the vehicle to a stop. This gave me a new respect for how difficult it is to control a car at high speed without one of the tires. Yet, on the trip home from Oklahoma, at night, with all passengers asleep, trucks surrounding me on three sides and a deep ravine on the fourth side, another tire blew. Miraculously, I managed to again bring the car to a stop without accident or injury. When I did, I stepped out of the car, fell to my knees, and thanked God for saving our lives, and I promised to serve God for the rest of my life.

Howard University

After graduating from Hales Franciscan High School in Chicago, I started college at Howard University in Washington, DC, determined to make a difference in the world. College was good for me in that it helped me to grow in confidence and become a more outgoing person. But it didn't work out quite the way I expected.

I went to college hoping to become a dentist. In my naïve, self-focused youthful mind, this was a way for me to make lots of money. However, during my freshman year in college, I noticed that I was frequently drowsy. As I moved through my sophomore and junior years of college, I found it nearly impossible to remain alert during my classes. It finally became clear that my dreams of starting dental school and eventually a successful dental practice were not going to happen. These debilitating bouts with drowsiness made it impossible for me to perform at a satisfactory level in the class-room.

Following a series of health challenges and financial hardship, I returned to Chicago. For the next several years, I struggled with sleep deprivation and day-time drowsiness.[20] I usually only got three hours of sleep a night. I was baffled, but I couldn't seem to control what was happening. Motivated by my desire to finish college, I worked several jobs.

Confused and afraid, I sought help from the Lord. The grandson and son of ministers, I resisted the temptation to be angry with the Lord. My plight caused me to look to the gospel of Jesus Christ for grace and mercy during my time of need. It was during this dark period in my life that the Lord reassured me that He would use me for His glory.

Looking back now, I see that God used these series of events to redirect me from a plan that wasn't right for me into a plan that was. Far from being a roadblock, God used this interruption to change the trajectory of my life, and today I am so glad that He did. What I'm doing now is what I was designed to do.

My dad said to me, "Have a Plan A, a Plan B, a Plan C and so on. If one plan doesn't work, switch to your back up plan." Today I share that same message with the young people I mentor. I encourage them. "You have options," I tell them, because they do. No one is powerless.

---

[20]   Nearly ten years later I was finally diagnosed with narcolepsy.

The Ram in the Bush: Ruffin Freeman

Every time unexpected help shows up just when I needed it, I thank God for being right on time. I thank Him for providing me a *ram in the bush.*

Many learn of this story in Genesis 22 during their Sunday school classes. Abraham was asked by God to sacrifice (kill) his only child, his son, Isaac as proof of his level of faith in God as his provider. Although with a heavy heart, Abraham did not hesitate to do the will of God. Following God's instructions, he took his son to the mountaintop. Isaac trusted his father Abraham like Abraham trusted his Father, God. When they reached the top, Isaac noticed there was no sacrificial lamb to sacrifice. The biblical narrative continues in verse 8:

> *Abraham answered, "God will give us the lamb for the sacrifice, my son."*
>
> *So Abraham and his son went on together and came to the place God had told him about. Abraham built an altar there. He laid the wood on it and then tied up his son Isaac and laid him on the wood on the altar. Then Abraham took his knife and was about to kill his son.*[21]

Abraham was saddened but willing to make one of the greatest sacrifices a father can make—to give the life of his son, especially his only son. There are no experiences of man that God can't empathize with. God

---

[21]   Genesis 22:8-10 NCV

made a similar sacrifice when he gave us His Son, Jesus, as a living sacrifice for us all.

The outcome for Abraham was different than he expected. The narrative continues:

> *But the angel of the Lord called out to him from heaven, "Abraham! Abraham!"*
>
> *"Here I am," he replied.*
>
> *"Do not lay a hand on the boy," he said. "Do not do anything to him. Now I know that you fear God, because you have not withheld from me your son, your only son."*
>
> *Abraham looked up and there in a thicket he saw a ram caught by its horns. He went over and took the ram and sacrificed it as a burnt offering instead of his son. So Abraham called that place* The Lord Will Provide. *And to this day it is said, "On the mountain of the Lord it will be provided."*[22]

During times of trouble, God who was already present with me said, "I am here." God is always with His children, those who call Him Lord. This is the most important truth you need to remember, no matter what challenges you are faced with or asked to do. If His will is to provide you with a "ram in the bush", He will. Just when you think you are completely out of options. When you feel no hope, God steps in right on time and opens the door of provision, hope and opportunities. He provides a ram in the bush to assist you,

---

[22]   Genesis 22:11-14 NIV

to serve you. Your ram could be your neighbor or a stranger in a store.

My ram was Elder Ruffin Freeman III. A devoted husband and loving father, he would call when I needed to talk. Frequently, he would share God's love for me right at the moment I was discouraged or in despair. As a young father in need of wise counsel, I met Elder Freeman at South Shore Baptist Church. While serving as the Elder responsible for the Christian education department and the instructor for the new member's class, he was the first member of South Shore Baptist Church to invite my family to dinner. For the next 20 years, he told me God's plan for marriage, family and ministry. When I was a graduate student, it seemed like every time I was going through a difficult experience, I would receive a call from Elder Freeman. Proverbs 17:17 describes our relationship best: "A friend loves at all times, and a brother is born for adversity." (JUB) It was with his encouragement that I decided to write this book.

God has the solution, but He often uses His children to provide it. We were created to be of service to others, to be someone's ram when they need it, if we are able. Years ago, I remember a friend told me the following: One day his neighbor had to get her mother to work by 7:00 am but also needed to get her daughter to elementary school by 8:20 am. She said she was out of options at trying to figure out how to pull both off. My friend had just gotten in that evening. About the same time, it occurred to his neighbor to ask him for help. She came over and asked my friend for help. He said,

"Of course." He didn't mind. She kept thanking my friend and saying how she owed him. He assured her there was no need, for her not to worry about it. She gave him this long tight hug saying, "Thank you, you are my ram in the bush!"

Even though he moved from Chicago to Louisville, KY, Elder Freeman and I spoke on the phone nearly every day before he passed away in 2014. Whatever you do, remember to serve when you can. Like Ruffin Freeman, we must look for those opportunities to serve, to be available to help during a time of need. Christians should always be about our Father's business. We must never forget those occasions when a need was met right on time, when you needed it. Moreover, we should consider the reward to know you've helped someone else during their time of need. Sometimes we need a ram in our bush, but sometimes we must be the ram in someone else's bush.

Support in Crisis. Romell Williams Sr.

In 1996, I became a deacon at South Shore Baptist Church. I was also the President of the Men's Ministry. As such, I worked closely with Elder Romell Williams Sr. He was the church elder who oversaw the Men's Ministry. For years, Romell, other men and I met every Tuesday and Thursday mornings from 6:00 to 7:00 am to discuss how to build healthy families, how to be better husbands, and other topics of interest to men. We discussed a number of books including *Living By the Book* by Howard Hendricks, *Measure of a Man* by Gene

Getz, *How to Manage Your Money* by Larry Burkett, *Men's Fraternity* by Robert Lewis, *Every Man's Battle* by Stephen Arterburn, *The Power of Focus* by Jack Canfield and more. We built a safe place for men to open up. Everyone knew that what was shared in the room, stayed in the room.

Becoming a men's ministry leader was a journey for me. It was the Lord's sense of humor that I should lead anything. Despite extreme bouts with shyness over the years, I have found my way into leadership positions. However, when presented with those opportunities, I've sought to show myself to be dependable and trustworthy. Many times people don't know how to interpret my laid back approach, not realizing that I am laser focused. People think of leaders as the people who are out front, but I'm very behind the scenes. I have no desire to be in the spotlight. Years of being the kid in the corner has given me sensitivity to those who are overlooked and unnoticed.

Along the way, others have encouraged me to get out there and lead in accordance with my gifting. Romell Williams Sr. was one of those people. Romell was a Chicago Police Officer and is a martial arts expert. He is both authoritative and compassionate; he has a heart for men. He is one of the most transparent men I know. If you don't want to hear the truth, don't ask Romell! Over the years of meeting together, we developed a deep friendship.

The value of that friendship was driven home on a cold December night in 1999. Two weeks after our youngest son was born, my wife complained of heartburn and stepped out to get some medicine at a local pharmacy. She was gone for what seemed an inordinate amount of time. Finally, the phone rang. A voice on the other end said to me, "Your wife had a heart attack. Her heart stopped for two minutes. You need to get here as soon as you can."

I found a babysitter for our young children and rushed to the hospital. For two hours I was unable to see her while the medical professionals attempted to stabilize her. She was hooked up to a ventilator and unconscious when I finally did see her.

Talk about a shock! My wife was 36 years old. We had been married for eight years. We didn't know at the time that there was a history of heart disease in the women of her family. Of the two of us, she's far more outgoing. I felt alone and isolated as I tried to come to terms with what just happened. In the midst of this scary experience, my sister-in-law said to me, "Why don't you call someone you know from your men's group." That gave me instant clarity. I immediately thought of Romell. He arrived at the hospital, it seemed, shortly after I hung up the phone even though it must have taken him some time because he lived some distance from where we were.

After his arrival, he remained at my side until 5:30 am when he needed to leave for work. I can't recall any-thing that he said, but his presence and his reassurance at that time meant everything to me. My wife suffered a second though milder heart attack three months later.

She went on to recover completely and is in good health today.

Romell continues to be a friend. When I go through times of discouragement, he is there for me. When donations for my ministry lag in a slow economy, he is right there reminding me of how important my work is.

During the darkest moment in my life, Romell left the warmth of his home on a cold December night to provide wise counsel and support when I needed him the most. He was able to make a difficult time much easier. I have never and will never forget his unselfish and unconditional love and support.

Recently, Romell and I attended the funeral of Elder Ruffin Freeman, a mentor that we both looked up to, an elder who counseled and encouraged both of us. Elder Freeman knew my gifts and encouraged me to be who I was-not what other people expected me to be. He also helped Romell and his wife to rebuild and strengthen their marriage during a time when that marriage relationship was strained.

My Uncle

My uncle, Rev. James E. Robinson is another example of the guiding hands of a mentor. A man of integrity and accomplishment, my uncle NEVER mentioned his achievements. Whenever I had the privilege of entering a room he was in, he was always interested in my thoughts and interests. In the 1960's, he marched with and was jailed with Dr. Martin Luther King Jr. during civil rights campaigns in Birmingham, Alabama. He was president of the Fairfield, Alabama NAACP from 1962-66. My uncle also served as lecturer and consultant for religious, educational and civic groups. However, it was his service to his family that challenged me to re-evaluate my life.

I traveled with my family to Augusta, Georgia to honor him on his 90th birthday. After so many years of serving others, my uncle completely amazed me by rising early on his 90th birthday and cooking and serving breakfast to my family. This act of service motivated me to ask myself, "Am I living a life of service to others? If a ninety-year-old man can continue to serve, why can't I?"

To be an effective mentor, you must be willing to serve. Two quotations come to mind:

> *"As each has received a gift, use it to serve one another, as good stewards of God's varied grace:"*
> 1 Peter 4:10 ESV

> *"Everyone can't be great, but everyone can serve."*
> Dr. Martin Luther King, Jr.

Dr. Dwight Perry

Often the reason people become mentors is because of the input or advice they receive from their own mentors. This certainly has been true in my life.

I discovered and clarified my life's mission as a result of mentoring I received from Dr. Dwight Perry, an author, educator, pastor, denominational leader and national speaker. In 2004 Dr. Perry and I were ministering at the same church. For two years I served as the President of the Men's Ministry while Dr. Perry was the Administrative Pastor. Our church had completed a 40-day fast. During this special time of prayer and fasting, I had been seeking God for direction on what to do with my life. At that time, I was a manager for a major pharmacy chain, but I felt this was not making the best use of my potential. I felt God was leading me and shaping me to do something other than being a manager. I felt like this wasn't what God had for me, that He wanted to use me in a more personal way to make a difference in many lives. My prayer was, "Show me the direction in which You want me to go."

When I expressed this to Dr. Perry, he took time out of his busy schedule to meet with me. Not only did he meet with me, he patiently listened as I described to him the crossroad I had reached. In spite of keeping a very rigorous schedule, he never looked at his watch or appeared rushed to get to his next appointment. I will never forget his example and his contribution to my life.

During our meeting, I shared my resume with Dr. Perry as well as the results of a spiritual gifts assessment. (I had scored highly in mercy and administration.) During our church fast, I had read *The Purpose Driven Life* by Rick Warren. To re-examine the direction of my life, I focused on Pastor Warren's SHAPE inventory: (1) spiritual gifts, (2) heart, (3) ability, (4) personality, and (5) experiences. It came into focus that I was gifted to be a mentor rather than a pastor. Dr. Perry used a similar inventory to assess my strengths and potential. As Dr. Perry listened he suggested that I consider pursuing a Master of Arts in Community Development at North Park University.

It is because of the integrity of Dr. Perry and his wise guidance that I discovered my life's mission. And Dr. Perry continues to speak into my life.

North Park University

With my interest piqued, I began researching and evaluating the program at North Park. I submitted an application, but after I was accepted, I had to tell the admissions department that I had no way of paying for this education. But God provided a way. The school put together a financial aid package that enabled me to pay for the program. God seemed to orchestrate all of the circumstances, and a couple years later I had earned my Master of Arts in Community Development in 2006.

My initial goal had been to resurrect a church/parachurch ministry known as Impact Ministries. This program was similar to the after school tutoring program provided by Sue Duncan. Since I had benefited from her Center, I was interested in creating something similar. As things evolved, however, it became clear that God had a different direction for me. I narrowed my focus to mentoring boys and young men, and started my own nonprofit organization, the Center for Community Development, NFP (CCD) in 2004.

I began to see how all the pieces were fitting together: my gifts of mercy and administration, combined with my experiences with my dad, Sue Duncan, men's ministry, basketball coaching, and Hales Fransciscan High School, placed in the context of my community where fathers are absent, more often than not, in a child's life. Mentoring encompasses both teaching and counseling. It allows me to put myself in the shoes of the person I'm working with. There was a need to go far beyond just helping with homework, and my background equipped me to do that. Mentoring just made sense. It was the right thing to do.

What Is a Mentor?

A mentor is someone who provides guidance and direction for someone who is younger or less experienced. A mentor is also someone who enters a voluntary relationship of trust and mutual respect with another person.

It is important to note that there is no specific method for mentoring. Every mentor is different, and each man who will mentor a boy will be different from anyone else. Each man will structure his mentoring relationship, shaping it according to his personality, gifts and abilities and his personal experiences.

Origin of Mentoring

The origins of mentoring go back to the Greek epic poem by Homer, *The Odyssey*. In the poem, Odyssey was sent to fight in the Trojan War. He left his son, Telemachus, in the care of a friend named Mentor. Mentor was Telemachus's caregiver and tutor. From these early origins, the name Mentor has become associated with a wise and supportive adviser. As a result, a mentor is someone who is an adviser, teacher, role model, and friend.

Example of General / President Grant

The life of Ulysses S. Grant illustrates the significant contribution a father or mentor can have on the life of a young person. Ulysses had grown up with a kind father. His father was a prosperous businessman during a time when men were struggling to make a living farming. The success of his father, Jesse Grant, allowed him to attend the best schools in his area. Unlike most boys Ulysses lived a carefree life. He had no ambition or passion for anything. He was so confused that friends called him "useless." As he approached the threshold of manhood, his father made a decision that would dramatically impact his life. Jesse Grant decided to send his son to West Point Military Academy, even though Ulysses did not want to go. However, when Ulysses returned home for the first time, it was clear that he had been transformed. The structure and discipline at West Point changed him. His friends stopped calling him "useless." As he indicated in his autobiography, Ulysses

S. Grant owed all the success he achieved in his life to his father. Grant used the instructions he received from West Point to win the Civil War and become president of the United States.

Growing Up with a Father in the Home Impacts the Outcome

Corbin played basketball with Nathan. While Nathan was physically larger, Corbin was much more aggressive. He was a go-getter. Did Corbin live an idyllic life? Far from it. Several of his peers were shot and killed. One of his teammates was shot on five different occasions before finally being murdered. (I attended his funeral in the South Shore community in Chicago.) But, despite these challenges, Corbin took his go-getter personality and applied it to life outside the basketball court. He attended a career academy for a year after high school. Then he entered a career in retail management where he excelled and remained steadily employed.

What was the difference? Two young men—same neighborhood, same basketball team, had vastly different outcomes. The answer is simple. Corbin grew up in a family where his dad was part of the home. Corbin's dad, a police officer, gave him guidance and the added push he needed to grow up and become a man. Nathan did not have a father in his home. In one home, the "blessing" was passed from father to son. In the other home, no dad was present to pass on that blessing.

Only a man can teach a boy how to be a man.

In my own case, I received a great deal of affirmation from my dad. He was always encouraging. Whatever dreams I concocted, he was supportive. He never said, "I don't think you can do that." Instead he said the opposite. "I think you can do that." Once I called my dad to tell him I was being asked to be a deacon. His response: "I'm not surprised." Even though my parents divorced, my dad never said a negative word about my mom. In fact, he recognized my mother's strengths and encouraged me to emulate them.

Escaping Violence; On Track for Employment as a Result of Mentoring

So what do we do for young men who have no father? We mentor!

A few years ago, I served as a mentor for Tristan. His mother found me and requested my assistance in mentoring him. When I met Tristan, his mother was concerned that he had no positive male role models in his life. The males in his life were either involved in street gangs, or they were incarcerated. In addition, because shootings were taking place at his high school in Chicago, his mother was concerned that he would become a victim of this deadly violence. He enrolled in Lincoln's Challenge Academy, a federal and state funded, military-type alternative education program situated on the site of the former Chanute Air Force Base two hours south of Chicago. One of the reasons why this program has been so successful is that each student is required to have a mentor. Mentors help students create a life plan, and work with them to transition from the structured setting of high school to the less structured setting of college and employment back in their home communities.

I drove to Rantoul, Illinois to meet with Tristan regularly. My own mentoring curriculum was combined with the expectations and guidelines of Lincoln's Challenge Academy to help him through school and transition back to Chicago. Every time I met with him, he seemed grateful that someone cared enough to take the time to meet with and mentor him.

Recently, I reached out to Tristan. He was grateful for the mentoring he received and said how helpful it was to him. He said it made him a better man. Today, at age 23, he's in the Job Corps working toward a job in the electrical trade. He's currently praying that he will get into an advanced training program with the railroad where he hopes to build a career.

Benefits of Mentoring

Mentoring programs are successfully changing the lives of young people. According to the Office of Juvenile Justice and Delinquency Prevention,[23] young people experienced the following outcomes as a result of partici-

---

[23] The Office of Juvenile Justice and Delinquency Prevention (OJJDP) helps state and local government to implement effective prevention and intervention programs.

pating in a mentoring program:

- initiating drug use: down 45.8%

- initiating alcohol use: down 27.4%

- violent behavior: down 31.7%

- school grades: up 3%

- scholastic competence: up 4.3%

- skipped class: down 36.7%

- skipped day of school: down 52.2%

Mentors are guiding lights in our society. Ask anyone with a history of accomplishments, and you can usually trace those achievements back to the guidance and support provided by a mentor. The contributions of one or more caring individuals are at the foundation of nearly all productive and successful lives.

Among other things, mentors help young people to enter college, go the distance and earn their degrees. Ronald Mincy, professor of social work at Columbia University and editor of *Black Males Left Behind*,[24] believes that we need more programs to help men enter and succeed in college. The programs are necessary because we live in a society where higher education is essential to economic success.

We must establish educational programs to help men enter and graduate from college, in order to end the poverty and family dysfunction our communities have

---

[24]   Urban Institute Press, 2006

been experiencing. In the Chicago area, the University of Illinois at Chicago is helping this process by sponsoring the Gaining Early Awareness and Readiness for Undergraduate Program (GEARUP) to help low-income middle school students prepare for college.

A Mentor Providing an Example of Fatherhood

Donald and his mother were members of my church. I promised my pastor that I would mentor Donald. My dad taught me that when you make a promise, you keep it. So beginning with his first year in high school, I spent time with him, playing catch, grabbing a Coke together—finding those teachable moments where I could speak into his life. Although he had a father, his father was not a regular part of his life. I knew I couldn't replace his dad and explained that to him, I wasn't trying to be his dad, but more like an older brother sharing life experiences with him. No, I wasn't going to sit down and lecture him for an hour because he already gets that in school. Instead, I said "this is going to be an exchange. I'm going to learn from you, and hopefully you're going to learn from me."

As time went on, circumstances arose with Donald, where he and his family had no place to live. So I moved him, his mother and his sister into our home with my wife and three sons where they lived for about a year and a half while Donald finished high school. I told his mom of my promise to be a role model for him. What better way to do that than to provide him and his family with a place to live in their time of need.

While I understood I wouldn't be perfect, I did seek to be authentic.

Recently, I reconnected with Donald who at the age 26 is now a father himself. When asked about his thoughts about that season of his life, he began by thanking me again for spending the time to teach him how to drive and for giving him his first vehicle. He recalled how I had introduced him to the sport of golf. He said, "I admired the example of fatherhood that you displayed in front of me. I've applied that experience to my family as well. I can't forget the constant motivation and father-like presence you displayed knowing that [my father] was not present ... I applaud and thank you for your mentorship." Donald has embraced the role of being a father. The generational cycle of fatherless homes—for him—has been broken.

Preparing Young Men for their Role as Fathers and Leaders

There are many children who live in father-absent homes. This is a contributing factor to the dysfunction that results in the homes of these children later in life. Fathers equip their children with the tools they will need later in life. In an ideal community you will find men mentoring boys leading to a more stable future for the family and the community. Mentoring is a means to develop better skills in boys through the talents and experiences of men in their lives. Young men will be given an opportunity to gain valuable skills through programs that educate, equip and engage them for their roles as fathers and leaders.

The Importance of Single Gender (Male) Mentoring

Boys need male leadership. They need male role models. While women (moms, teachers, tutors, sisters, leaders and friends) do fill an important role in a boy's life, only a man can teach a boy how to be a man. Some of the most successful educational programs in the inner city acknowledge and build on this reality. One hundred percent of the students at the all-male Hales Franciscan High School who graduated went on to college. By contrast, only one in four African American males in Chicago public schools graduated from high school.

Tim King, former president of Hales Franciscan, used this understanding to launch Urban Prep Charter Academy, an all-boys public high school in Chicago's South Side Englewood neighborhood in 2006.[25] King understands that boys learn differently than girls, and respond well to the right kind of pressure. With Urban Prep, he has created a highly structured environment with low student-to-staff ratios and a high proportion of male African American teachers and administrators. Kate N. Grossman, Education Reporter for the Chicago *SunTimes* reports, "The idea is to create a sense of community and brotherhood and give the boys enough support so they know their teachers truly want

---

[25] See Grossman, Kate N., "A bold plan to set black boys up for success." *Chicago SunTimes.* 9/3/2006. http://www.highbeam. com/doc/1P2-1641222.html accessed 12/1/2014.

them to succeed."

Both students and teachers appreciate the difference. Thankful that someone raised the bar for him, one freshman said, "Here, you feel like you're someone important." A teacher expressed gratitude that there were no "power struggles" with the students.

In Philadelphia, the Sankofa Passages Program, placed Black and Latino boys with male mentors inside the schools where they met three times a day, five days a week.[26] Before starting the program, most of these boys could not identify a single positive male role model in their lives. When asked who their male role model was, many of them answered, "my mother." Although the 352 students in the program were at risk with multiple social and emotional needs, 63 of 65 seniors in the program in the spring of 2014 graduated. The mentors were minority men, many of whom had overcome tremendous early challenges in order to be successful in life. They worked hard to empower their mentees to become even more successful than they had been. An important part of the program was creating a safe place for boys to share their stories without judgment. Mentors pointed to the importance of being listened to, something that sometimes gets overlooked in the educational process. There was freedom for mentors to cover the life skills that aren't taught in a typical academic curriculum—life skills as varied as hygiene,

[26] See Farr, Stephanie, "The sinking of Sankofa." Philadelphia *Daily News*, 9/23/2014 http://articles.philly.com/2014-09-24/news/54244360_1_mentors-role-model-latino accessed 12/1/2014.

how to tie a tie, how to interact with the police, how to treat women, how to respond to injustice. Much of the mentoring centered around overcoming negative and cynical thinking with productive and positive thoughts. Students were empowered to take charge over their futures. With many of the boys being raised in single mother households, having a positive male role model was key. These young men came to understand that other people believed in them and were counting on them to succeed. Male mentors were important because many times teachers were unwilling or unable to provide the mentoring that students needed. Mentors also helped students process grief, loss and crises. Tragically, the program was cut due to lack of funding.

Open and Honest

I mentored Brandon while he was a student at Hales Franciscan High School. He was an interesting, personable, hardworking and driven young man, his parents were not in the picture. I did not know the details of his situation, or what happened to his parents, I just know that a legal guardian was caring for him.

Brandon, who is now a freshman at a college in the South, emailed me recently, and said, "I learned a lot from you and the other Hales Franciscan mentors during my junior and senior years of high school … I enjoyed being open and honest with the mentors, and the program was always a success."

Ongoing Relationships

To past mentees, I am always available providing references for jobs, and responding to their questions and concerns. When a former mentee has something that he can't share with anyone else, he comes to me because we still have that level of trust in our relationship. This goes back to my dad and me, and the level of trust we had.

Determine the Assets:

A First Step Toward a Solution

To deal with the crisis that exists in our city, one of the first things needed is a determination of the assets that exist within our community. After we have completed this inventory of our capabilities, we are in a position to bring solutions the community. While mentoring is not limited to Christians, in the African American community, the church has historically been central to the culture. The church has helped to inform our community of our core values, providing guidance for that bedrock of character that is so important in the life of a young man. In an ideal community, Christian men use their unique gifts and skills to mentor boys. You will find these Christian men of all educational and economic backgrounds teaching, guiding and counseling boys, investing themselves in the lives of the boys in their church and in their community.

Mentoring Strategies

One size does NOT fit all, and different approaches to mentoring at different times in a person's life are needed to achieve the right kind of results for the community.

Five Common Mentoring Environments

Mentoring can take place in a number of environments. Here are some of the more common embodiments:

- *Community-based mentoring* which include programs like Big Brothers, Big Sisters, YMCA, and Boys and Girls Clubs.

- *Faith-based mentoring* brings biblical and spiritual emphasis into the mentoring process and is most commonly associated with a church or para-church ministry.

- *School-based mentoring* programs typically emphasize academic achievement and college preparation.

- *Work-based mentoring* helps young people to learn basic workplace skills and to identify postgraduate goals.

- *Site-based mentoring* which includes programs like the Sue Duncan Children's Center and Cabrini Connections.

Faith-based and School-based Mentoring

Over the years I've done both faith-based and school-based mentoring.

School-based mentoring programs offer several advantages. For one, mentors have access to a larger number of protégées. Mentors also have access to teachers of students they are mentoring. This allows mentors to obtain another perspective on the person(s) they are working with. It's always easier to do a better job when you're working with more information. School based programs are excellent platforms for exposing young people to career options, and can also be used for character building. The young people I've worked with in school-based programs are curious, not fully mature, looking to find their purpose in life and open to new ideas—making them easier to work with.

Faith-based mentoring programs likewise offer unique advantages. Working from a common spiritual foundation, when mentors and mentees have the same point of reference with respect to moral issues, this allows the mentoring relationship to move forward with fewer hindrances. "Love your neighbor" means something specific to a young person who has grown up in a church environment. Faith-based programs also bring a biblical focus into the relationship, which allows mentors to be open and honest with mentees about important segments of their journey.

Growing up as a preacher's kid, in my mind there was no separation between faith and all other aspects of life. I came to see how everything is connected to God.

61

In a faith-based mentoring relationship, if the two parties attend the same church, there is a common frame of reference in the programming of the church. A mentor may point to a recent sermon or Sunday school lesson to more effectively illustrate a point.

Four Forms of Mentoring

While we may think of mentoring as typically occurring in a one-to-one relationship, this is one of several possibilities. The four most common approaches are:

- One-to-one mentoring represents the traditional method where one more experienced person is matched with a lesser experienced individual. It can also be one youth paired with a more experienced peer.

- Team mentoring. This form matches a group of adults with a group of youth in a structured setting.

- Group mentoring involves one or two adult volunteers developing a relationship with a group of youth through regular meetings. The Girl Scouts and Boy Scouts are examples of group mentoring.

- Three-tier mentoring is a form of mentoring in which a wise older person mentors an individual, while that individual maintains an accountability[27] relationship with a peer (peer mentoring), and mentors a younger person. In the bible, Paul had a three-tier relationship with Barnabas and Timothy; David had a peer mentoring relationship with Jonathan.

I have included a resource guide for several mentoring organizations. (See Appendix A.)

Components of Effective Mentoring

Some of the components of an effective mentoring program may include:

- Recruitment: Recruit appropriate mentors and mentees by realistically describing the program's aims and expected outcomes.

- Screening: Screen prospective mentors to determine whether they have the time, commitment and personal qualities to be an effective mentor. Conduct comprehensive criminal background checks on adult mentors including checking sex offender and child abuse registries.

- Training: Train prospective mentors in the basic knowledge and skills needed to build an effective mentoring relationship.

- Matching: Match mentors and mentees along dimensions likely to increase the odds that

---

[27] That is, someone who holds you accountable for achieving your goals.

mentoring relationships will endure.

- Monitoring and Support: Monitor mentoring relationship milestones and support mentors with ongoing advice, problem-solving support and training opportunities for the duration of the relationship.

- Closure: Facilitate bringing the match to closure in a way that affirms the contributions of both the mentor and the mentee and offers both individuals the opportunity to assess the experience.

Additional Services for Mentors

- A service that provides news and other information relevant to men's issues, advice for men to improve their skills as fathers, husbands and community leaders.

- Support groups within the community to assist men in developing a relationship with their children.

- Access to interactive media to give men information and advice on how to be more involved in their children's lives.

- Partnerships with churches that offer a variety of programs for men such as GED, job training and bible study.

A Mentor's Responsibility

What is the mentor's responsibility to their mentee? A mentor should help the mentee to believe in himself and boost his confidence. Mentors should ask challenging questions, while providing guidance and encouragement. Mentoring allows the mentee to explore new ideas with confidence. This relationship provides the mentee with an opportunity to look closely and honestly at himself, his issues, his opportunities and the goals he sets for life. Mentoring empowers mentees to take responsibility for their lives and guiding their lives in the direction they decide, rather than leaving things to chance. A mentor is an adviser who helps the mentees to discover the right direction and develop solutions to life issues. Mentors use similarities in life experiences to establish lasting relationships with young persons. Moreover, mentoring provides mentees with opportunities to think about their life options.

Effective mentors:

- share critical knowledge.

- teach by example.

- offer wise counsel.

- set high expectations of performance.

- listen to personal problems.

- confront negative behaviors and attitudes.

- provide growth experiences.

- help build self-confidence.

- inspire their mentees.

Matching Mentors and Mentees

As we match mentors and mentees we seek to find the kind of commonality that creates the best opportunities for building a lasting relationship. We do take into account ethnic background, hobbies and interests, life experience, motivation for being in a mentoring relationship, and personality. We ask potential mentors and mentees to describe themselves using words such as quiet, shy, nervous, withdrawn, outgoing, talkative, friendly, insecure, inquisitive, adventuresome, confident, spiritual, sensitive, happy, moody. One question we ask mentors is, "What were you like in junior high?" We also determine whether mentors are interested in helping mentees in business, education, social skills or all three. We try to determine what kind of commitment both the mentor and mentee are prepared to give to the program. We don't want mentees to form a relationship with a mentor who can't be there for at least a year and can't spend at least a couple hours a month with the mentee.

A Typical Mentoring Session

While every mentoring session will be as unique as the

individuals involved, here's a format we follow in our school-based group mentoring program.

Typically we have 5-15 mentees and 2-3 mentors[28] in the room.

We usually begin our biweekly one-hour long session with an ice breaker. It might be something as simple as "my favorite food is... [fill in the blank]." Then we give time for each mentee to share anything they wish from a recent experience. This gives group members an opportunity to catch up, to vent, to "get real" in a safe atmosphere where mentees know other group members care about them. Mentees receive support and advice for the problems they face.

Realistically, young men are often reluctant to share their deepest issues and may not share anything at all. That's understandable. Most live in an environment where it's not safe to be vulnerable and share that kind of information. No problem; we just keep working to make it safe, and little by little, mentees become more open and honest. Mentors may ask questions to generate a response, but do so only in a way that allows everyone to feel safe.

Sometimes a mentor will suggest a life skill topic. For example, a mentor might say, "I'm not going to ask you to raise your hand, but maybe you need help filling out

---

[28] Having 2-3 mentors in the room takes the pressure off any one person, and also allows the mentees to feel more comfortable, and to establish a closer rapport with at least one of the mentors. It also provides a level of accountability so there's no question about any impropriety.

a check. By the time we're done today, you'll know how to do that."

Then we move into our educational component—the official topic of the day. In our Steps to Manhood curriculum, we cover twenty attributes of leadership. This is a character development curriculum specifically designed for a school-based mentoring program. In a faith-based mentoring program, we cover similar topics, but with different vocabulary and emphasis. For example, "twenty attributes of leadership" might be "traits of a godly man." We make sure there's a relevant "take away" for everyone.

None of this is done in lecture form—it is all accomplished through dialogue. Along the way, when we find teachable moments, we weave in life skills and life lessons. While talking we may, for example, discover that one of the mentees applied for a job, but was not sure if how they went about it was appropriate. That could lead to a discussion of image, dress, how to ask for a job, how to interview, how to fill out an application and so on.

At the end of our meeting, one of the mentors does a bullet-point recap of the meeting and reminds everyone of the next scheduled meeting. As an incentive to keep mentees involved, we may offer a prize—a gift card or a pizza party for example—if mentees show up for so many sessions on time.

On occasion, we might use our time for an outing or "field trip." For example, we might do "legal career day" and visit a law firm, or "medical career day" and visit a hospital and so on.

Throughout this process, mentors keep in mind that mentees need to be affirmed in a positive way.

A faith-based mentoring session is similar in most respects. However, the educational module may be different. For example, it may be based on a passage of scripture. In one program, we went through the book of Proverbs. We may open with prayer as well as an ice-breaker, and close in prayer. Typically the faith-based mentoring programs I've been involved in have involved smaller groups, generally one adult mentor with two or three young men as mentees. Because these environments are usually closer to a one-to-one ratio, deeper relationships are often formed. I've made a point of letting my mentees know that if they need me after the program is over, I am available.

What Are the Qualifications Needed for Mentoring?

Do you need to be a highly outgoing type of person to be a mentor? Not necessarily. In my case, I'm more of an introvert, but I still enjoy close and rewarding relationships with the young men that I mentor. I've seen a variety of personalities function well as mentors.

Do you need to have a master's degree in education? No.

The only requirement for this mentoring relationship is the willingness to get to know one boy and take the time to do it. The primary purpose of mentoring is to come alongside and simply be there for a boy.

Relationship is the key qualification. Mentors must be committed to a relationship.

I have noticed, however, that people who have been mentored understand the importance of mentoring, and are usually more willing to step into that role. People who have not been mentored have trouble conceptualizing that role and how it could be beneficial to the mentee, to themselves and to the community. Mentoring tends to take them out of their comfort zone. This lack of experience can be overcome; it just takes a little more work.

The Role of the Church

In an ideal community, the church equips men for building communities. The church lays the spiritual foundation and values for men. Men build on the foundation by creating programs to help boys grow into manhood. This might come in the form of men organizing boys in the community to participate in positive meaningful intellectual and physical activities— chess/checker clubs, summer basketball tournaments, and open gym time at local parks or churches. During these activities, men build positive relationships with boys and give them an alternative to hanging out on street corners.

This means that the church must lead the way in providing a different view of men. Currently, men have an insignificant role in the family and in the community. Men are told that they are not needed. The church has an important role in turning this around. In the bible, Moses gives this instruction to men:

> *You shall teach them [your children] diligently to your children, and shall talk of them when you sit in your house, when you walk by the way, when you lie down, and when you rise up.*[29]

In an ideal community, men will mentor boys, diligently teaching them day and night. They will teach them by precept and example. Precepts will come from a written text. Examples will come from the lives of the mentors put on display.

How will we know that this ideal community is being developed? Our goal will be reached when we see a significant increase in the number of children growing up with involved, responsible, and committed men in their lives.

One challenge is that the church is no longer central to the African American culture and community. Many people, particularly younger people have walked away from church after experiencing or observing something negative. Financial mismanagement, abuse of power or infidelity on the part of a church leader may cause some people—understandably—to lose respect for the church. Good pastors and other church leaders are working hard to overcome these challenges, but this reality must be faced.

---

[29]   Deuteronomy 6:7 NKJV

Starting the Center for Community Development and the Steps to Manhood Mentoring Program

Inspired by a wealth of information and the passion of my instructor, Susan Rans, during my first semester in the North Park University's Master of Arts in Community Development program (MACD), I watered the seed of service planted by my great-great-grandfather, and started my own community organization, Center for Community Development, NFP. CCD is a 501c(3) non-profit organization committed to the development of youth, the empowerment of men, and the promotion of economic development.

I selected the name, Center for Community Development (CCD), because my roots are in the church and I believe that the church should be the center for community development. During my youth, the church was the center of activity in the community. Day care, employment resources, and adult education could be obtained in the church.

The central focus of CCD is the Steps to Manhood mentoring program. I developed this to offer hope to boys and young men through training in life skills, character development, financial literacy, and entrepreneurship. The Steps to Manhood program strategically challenges students to identify and reach their goals. With the assistance of a mentor, students create a plan of action to make dreams become reality. This frequently goes full circle as some of our mentors of today were themselves mentored early in the program.

Conclusion

I hope I've inspired you to consider the role you can play in mentoring.

Many people look at the multitude of problems plaguing our urban centers and throw up their hands thinking that there's no hope. Crime and violence have escalated almost out of control. The state of the family is dismal. Poverty, decay and hopelessness abound. But there is hope. There are simple strategic steps all of us can take to transform a culture. The key is mentoring.

Any person of integrity can be a mentor. No special qualifications are needed. You don't need to possess a college degree. You don't need to be a certain personality type. You don't need to be an educator, a pastor, a business leader, or any kind of professional. You simply need to be there for another person. You may not have all the answers; in fact, you won't. But you can model a life of integrity to an impressionable young protegee. You can let someone else know that you care. Every person needs to know that he matters, and you can send that message. You can encourage. You can listen. You can support. You can help.

The need for mentors is particularly acute in the African American community where the percentage of children being raised by single moms is far higher than the national average. Only a man can teach a boy how to be a man. When fathers are absent, surrogate fathers —mentors—step in and fill the gap. Even when fathers are present or partially present, mentors still fill a vital role. This is why male mentors, particularly African

American male mentors are so desperately needed.

Even if you're not male and not African American, you can still make an important difference. You can tutor. You can mentor in the context of your own community. You can raise awareness and support for effective inner city mentoring programs. You can become an advocate for mentoring. You can support and encourage good people who are on the front lines making a difference.

As you process the contents of this book and ponder how you can best get involved, I would love to connect with you and help you in any way that I can. Please contact me through my website:

www.cfcdevelopment.com

James E. Warren

Center for Community Development NFP (a 501c3 corporation)

December 2014

Appendix A:

Mentoring Organizations

CHICAGO-AREA MENTORING ORGANIZA-TIONS

Big Brothers Big Sisters of Metropolitan Chicago
560 W. Lake St 5th FL
Chicago, IL 60661
312-427-0637
www.bbbschgo.org
Big Brothers
Big Sisters of Metropolitan Chicago has been serving Cook County since 1969, and is one of 500 agencies nationwide striving to aid in the positive development of our youth. Nearly 700 volunteers remain the backbone of our program by serving as friends, mentors, and role models; all to help children build self-confidence.

100 Black Men of Chicago
2929 S. Wabash Ave Suite 201
Chicago, IL 60616
www.100bmc.org
100 Black Men of Chicago was formed in November of 1994 and subsequently incorporated in December of 1995 by a group of men who shared a common goal of providing youth with educational and mentoring opportunities, with particular emphasis on young African American males.

YMCA of Metropolitan Chicago

801 North Dearborn Street
Chicago, IL 60610
312-932-1200
800-514-1224
www.ymcachgo.org

The YMCA of Metropolitan Chicago's youth programs help children and teenagers realize their abilities, make healthy choices, and develop leadership skills. Over the last year, the YMCA served more than 6,000 youth from the city and the suburbs, who spent more than 200,000 hours in our programs.

Boy Scouts of America

Chicago Area Council
1218 W. Adams St
Chicago, IL 60607
312-421-8800
www.chicagobsa.org

The mission of the Boy Scouts of America is to prepare young people to make ethical and moral choices over their lifetimes by instilling in them the values of the Scout Oath and Law.

Boys and Girls Clubs of Chicago

Has 31 Locations in Chicago
www.bgcc.org

Boys and Girls Clubs of Chicago Mentoring – Sponsored by the Regenstein Foundation, our mentoring program pairs Boys & Girls Clubs members with an adult mentor. Mentors and mentees spend up to two hours each week at the Club to work on homework, shoot hoops, work on craft projects, play foosball or just talk.

TALKS Mentoring

P.O. Box 111
Champaign, IL 61824-0111
217-352-4628
dr.harolddavis@talksmentoring.org
Dr. Harold Davis, founded the TALKS Mentoring Program in 1995. TALKS (Transfer A Little Knowledge Systematically) Mentoring uses the three tier mentoring method.

Tutor/Mentor Connection

Online Resource for locating Chicago-Area tutoring and mentoring programs:
http://www.tutormentorprogramlocator.net/Prgloc.aspx
The mission of the Tutor/Mentor Connection (T/MC)* is to gather and organize all that is known about successful non-school tutoring/mentoring programs and apply that knowledge to expand the availability and enhance the effectiveness of these services to children throughout the Chicago region.

See also http://www.tutormentorexchange.net to read more mentoring ideas from Dan Bassill.

NATIONAL MENTORING ORGANIZATIONS

Big Brothers Big Sisters of America
P.O. Box 141599
Irving, TX 75014
469-351-3100
http://www.bbbs.org

100 Black Men of America
141 Auburn Avenue
Atlanta, GA 30303
404-688-5100
http://www.100blackmen.org

YMCA of USA
101 N. Wacker Drive
Chicago, IL 60606
800-872-9622
http://www.ymca.net

Boys and Girls Clubs of America
1275 Peachtree Street NE
Atlanta, GA 30309-3506
404-487-5700
http://www.bgca.org

Appendix B:

Leaders Speak Out on Mentoring

Arne Duncan

In 2006, while a student at North Park University, I had the privilege of interviewing US Secretary of Education Arne Duncan[30] who was CEO of Chicago Public Schools at the time. During that interview, Mr. Duncan pointed to the impact that his mentor, John Rogers, Jr. (founder and chairman of Ariel Capital Management) had on his life. Mr. Duncan began mentoring professionally while working with the Ariel Foundation's I Have a Dream tutoring program. Of course, Mr. Duncan, son of Sue Duncan, is no stranger to tutoring and mentoring, as he worked closely with his mother's program while growing up. He conveyed to me that he is motivated by the desire to pass on to young people the values, work ethic and life lessons he gained as a result of the human interactions he has had with his family and friends. Mr. Duncan's parents were strong advocates of education. Having two parents in the home helped create a strong foundation for his life. The encouragement of his mentor helped Mr. Duncan to make the transition into a career in education following a professional basketball career in Australia.

---

[30] Personal interview with Arne Duncan on 9/12/2006.

Dr. Joseph Rhoiney

Dr. Joseph Rhoiney of Ministry ONE referred to statistics provided by mentoring.org to point to the need for mentors. Of the 35.2 million young people in the United States today, one out of four lives with a single parent. One youth in ten was born to teen parents. One out of five lives in poverty and one out of ten will not finish high school. Every young person, says Dr. Rhoiney, is at risk for something. Only through a combination of various protective factors (including mentoring) can youth be steered in a positive direction toward healthy development and adulthood.

By becoming a mentor, one can empower a beleaguered young person to feel a part of his or her community and to contribute to its development. Being a mentor helps kids broaden their views and offers them new experiences. Mentors, though, gain the satisfaction of seeing a child accomplish something they didn't think they could. The heart of it is the relationship. And it's a two-way street. What the mentee gets is confidence, significance, a sense of belonging, a hopeful outlook, and the motivation and skills to succeed. As for the older person, serving as a mentor gives one meaning, gives one purpose, and offers the profound satisfaction of making a lasting difference in a child's life.

Dr. Dwight Perry

Dr. Dwight Perry, national speaker and author, District Executive Pastor for Converge Great Lakes, former professor and pastor, points to the spiritual dimension and benefits of mentoring: "Mentoring is essential because it helps to transfer truth through the number one means available: real life examples touching other real lives. Mentoring allows us to see the truth of scripture worked out and worked through a real life person. It helps the person being mentored to have hope that just like God has worked in the life of the person who is doing the mentoring He can work in their life."

He continues, "I came to know Christ through a Christian organization known as the Navigators. They were and are famous for their one-to-one discipleship approach to growth. I was mentored from day one in my Christian experience by experienced and godly men who invested themselves in me and taught me both verbally and by their example the importance of me doing the same for others. The impact that I have seen mentoring have on my life personally and the other men that I have been around. The results cannot be argued against when true mentoring takes place around the transforming Word of God."

Milton Massey

Milton Massey, national/regional director for Here's Life Inner City Chicago, takes it a step further and says discipleship is a deeper form of mentoring that comes from a more committed relationship. He cites the examples of Paul, Barnabas and Timothy to show the importance of a three-tier relationship. Discipleship is the way to carry out the Great Commission. Mr. Massey adds this simple formula: rules without relationship = rebellion.

Pastor James Ford, Jr.

Pastor James Ford, Jr., Senior Pastor of Christ Bible Church of Chicago, puts it this way: "There are only two things that last forever, the Word of God and souls of men. Mentoring is not only teaching a life in time, it could also help save a soul for eternity." He conveyed his experience of growing up as the oldest of ten children with no positive male influence in his life. His mentor became his surrogate father. Mentoring "was part of what God used to turn my life totally around." He adds, "Mentoring is important because values and mores are better caught than taught. It not only takes teaching to communicate and nurture boys, it also takes time. As you spend time in normal everyday activities with mentees, they get a visible tangible model of what they could become." Mentors not only function as role models, but the closeness of the relationship can have a powerful positive impact on a young life.

Russell Knight

Russell Knight, founder of Chicago Urban Reconciliation Enterprise, was realistic about the challenges for setting up a mentoring program. Many times these programs don't get the support they need from pastors, and it can be challenging to find enough men who will commit themselves to mentoring in the long term. The best mentoring happens when men take young people everywhere they go. He pointed to the Scouts and to certain sports programs (e.g., basketball camps) as examples of well-run mentoring programs. He said that mentoring works best when the young person approaches the adult to request mentoring. Ideally, young men should be exposed to life outside their neighborhood. Men need to learn to be transparent and authentic with the boys they mentor.

To learn more about James E. Warren and the Center for Community Development, visit

www.cfcdevelopment.com

www.ingramcontent.com/pod-product-compliance
Lightning Source LLC
Chambersburg PA
CBHW071226280526
45787CB00002B/821